Discovering
Who You Are and
How God Sees You

H. NORMAN WRIGHT

AspirePress

Torrance, California

AspirePress

Discovering Who You Are and How God Sees You
Copyright © 2014 H. Norman Wright.
All rights reserved.
Aspire Press, an imprint of Rose Publishing, Inc.
4733 Torrance Blvd., #259
Torrance, California 90503 USA
www.aspirepress.com

Register your book at www.aspirepress.com/register

The views and opinions expressed in this book are those of the author(s) and do not necessarily express the views of Aspire Press, nor is this book intended to be a substitute for mental health treatment or professional counseling.

All scripture quotations, unless otherwise indicated, are taken from the Holy Bible, New International Version®, NIV®. Copyright ©1973, 1978, 1984, 2011 by Biblica, Inc.™ Used by permission of Zondervan. All rights reserved worldwide. www.zondervan.com The "NIV" and "New International Version" are trademarks registered in the United States Patent and Trademark Office by Biblica, Inc.™

Scripture quotations marked (NASB) taken from the New American Standard Bible®, Copyright © 1960, 1962, 1963, 1968, 1971, 1972, 1973, 1975, 1977, 1995 by The Lockman Foundation. Used by permission.

Scripture quotations marked (NLT) are taken from the Holy Bible, New Living Translation, copyright ©1996, 2004, 2007, 2013 by Tyndale House Foundation. Used by permission of Tyndale House Publishers, Inc., Carol Stream, Illinois 60188. All rights reserved.

Scripture quotations marked (TLB) are taken from The Living Bible, copyright ©1971. Used by permission of Tyndale House Publishers, Inc., Carol Stream, Illinois 60188. All rights reserved.

Printed in the United States of America
010914RRD

Contents

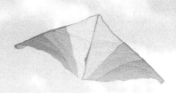

CHAPTER ONE

Searching for Identity

The car cruised by my house twice before the driver parked in front. It was several minutes before the driver emerged. She looked at her watch and then started toward the house. Everything about her said "money"—from her clothes and her jewelry to her late-model BMW. She came up the walkway in a confident, brisk manner. I didn't know much about her since our only conversation had been to set up an appointment to, as she said, "talk over a few items, nothing too significant." As she entered, I noticed that she was impeccably dressed, carried a chestnut Italian leather Dooney Bourke handbag, and wore jewelry that could have been designed by Judith Ripka. Her handshake was firm, and she chose her own chair in the office. But then her demeanor changed.

She sat there looking quite desolate, her face reflecting the sense of loss that stormed within her. Soon she began to put into words what was so obvious from her outward expression: "I thought I knew who I was. I've always seen myself as capable. I have a very prestigious career, which gives me a high status. I used to pride myself on that, but now it just doesn't seem enough. My job isn't fulfilling anymore. In the past if someone asked me, 'Who are you?' I could give them a great answer, but it was always tied to my position in the company. I thought that was better than what I used to base my identity on. When I was younger, it was my looks. I was attractive and I knew it. I worked on it to get the most mileage out of it. One day I realized that eventually no matter what I did to look good, it wouldn't help. Age would catch up with me, and then what would I have? Who would I be? But now I'm floundering again. I don't really know who I am, and I feel empty and depressed over it."

WHO ARE YOU?

Have you ever been there, in that bottomless pit where you wondered who you were and no answers came? When it happens, it is frightening. We all need to have some meaning for who we are.

Any of us can suffer a loss of identity, but it is a loss that in most cases is preventable. That's right: it can be prevented. Many identity losses are felt because the foundation we base our identity on is shaky.

Too often we think that striving for identity is a search done only when we are adolescents. Once we attain adulthood, it should be over, but it isn't. Think about it for a minute. What do you base your identity on? Don't you define yourself by your role, or what you do? Don't you establish who you are by your emotional attachments to other people, places and things? Or do you base it on your appearance? It is quite typical for people to do this, and that would be fine if life were static, certain, and always predictable—but it isn't.

Take a moment and write your response to this question: "Who are you?"

_____

_____

_____

_____

_____

_____

_____

What did you write? Did you discover you were responding with the roles you play in your life? Often I hear answers such as, "I am a man," "I am a father," "I am a minister," "I am a widower," "I am a family person," or "I am an athlete." But if you couldn't identify who you are by one of these roles, what would you say?

FRAGILE IDENTITIES

If we do not have a broad basis for our identity, any kind of loss may put our identity into question.

- ➤ Who will you be if you are no longer a father?

- ➤ Who will you be when you are no longer a social worker?

- ➤ Who will you be when you are no longer a minister?

- ➤ Who will you be when you are no longer an athlete?

- ➤ Who will you be if you can no longer run or walk?

- ➤ Who are the people you are attached to for your identity?

- ➤ What about your appearance? Does your identity fluctuate based on how well you think you look?

- ➤ What about your performance? Does how you feel about yourself fluctuate on the basis of your performance?

If we have no sense of who we are beyond our different roles in life or our emotional attachments, we have confined ourselves to a state of future identity confusion. However, it is possible for this loss to be avoided.

When we suffer a loss after having built our identity on anything that can change, we may experience the loss of our identity as well. Perhaps this startling fact will help us see how tenuous the foundation for our identity really is. Do you ever feel fragile? One counselee described herself as a thin china plate that could shatter at any moment.

When we're confused about who we are, it's hard to walk in the blessing of God.

We live in a time of fragile identities. I have heard people identify themselves and then suffer a loss that affects their identity:

➢ "I'm the president of a large company." (But the next week he filed for bankruptcy.)

- "I'm the coach of a winning college football team." (But this season the team lost six games, and he lost his job.)

- "I'm a model for a large department store chain." (But she was suddenly replaced by a model half her age.)

- "I'm a mother." (Yet this past year one of her children died and another ran away from home and hasn't been heard from since.)

- "I'm a concert pianist." (But two of his fingers were severed in an accident five days ago.)

So what happens to their identity now that a loss has taken place? Does it shatter? Was it too fragile? Was it built on society's easily breakable standards? Did it have a base that could not withstand the sudden and unexpected earthquakes of life?

At one of my seminars, I frustrate people because I ask them to introduce themselves to those around them and tell who they are without mentioning what they do for a living. Just that simple instruction puts many of them in a state of conflict. Many of them are frustrated because their identity is based primarily on what they do—their job, their role in the family, their role in the church.

Would you be frustrated too? Is your identity based on the physical and emotional elements of your existence? Are you someone who ought to wear a sign that says, "Fragile. Handle with care. I break easier than you think"? Not sure?

If we have no sense of who we are beyond our physical abilities and roles and emotional ties in life, we have confined ourselves to a state of identity confusion. And when we're confused about who we are, it's hard to walk in the blessing of God.

AVOIDING CONFUSION

You can avoid confusion by determining what you have based your identity on. *What things are you attached to that influence your identity?* For example, how important is your house, your job, your community standing, your car, and your wardrobe as sources for your identity?

Whenever we build our identity on anything that is potentially changeable, what do you think happens to our identity? It makes us prone to experiencing not only the changes and losses themselves but the potential loss of our identity as well.

> ➢ I've met beautiful women and handsome men who have felt like nobodies—no real identity.

> ➢ I've known wealthy men and women of all ages who have felt like nobodies—no real identity.

> ➢ I've seen men and women with power and prestige who have felt like nobodies—no real identity.

From the world's standpoint, these people have everything. But it doesn't matter. What they really have wanted has eluded them—their identity. They all have felt like the person in this song:

If I were a cloud, I'd sit and cry,
If I were the sun, I'd sit and sigh,
But I'm not a cloud, nor am I the sun,
I'm just sitting here, being no one.

If I were the wind, I'd blow here and there,
If I were the rain, I'd fall everywhere,
But I'm not the wind, nor am I the rain,
I'm just no one—feeling pain.

If I were the snow, I'd fall oh so gently,
If I were the sea, waves would roll o'er me,
But I'm not the snow, nor am I the sea,
I'm just no one . . .[1]

When are the times that you feel like "no one"? What does it take for this to occur?

CHAPTER TWO

Looking Deeper into Your Identity

YOUR WORK

Let's look deeper into the basis for your identity from the work you do.

Work is often used as the basis for our self-esteem. Self-esteem increases when we feel good about what we accomplish on the job. It is part of the performance basis for identity. Work becomes more than a source of income, even though some people will cling to the belief that money is really the main motivating factor of a job. But what happens if you are in a job that involves long-term projects with few visible indicators of how you are doing? What if you are in a sales job and each month you start over, having to meet your quota and compete against all the other salespeople? Situations such as these put the self-esteem of some people on a roller-coaster ride every month, offering little stability for their identity.

Where are you in this aspect of your life? Evaluate yourself on a scale of 0 to 10 as you consider the link between your self-esteem and your work:

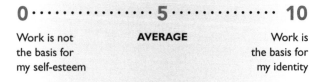

0 · · · · · · · · · · · · · · 5 · · · · · · · · · · · · 10
Work is not the basis for my self-esteem · · · · · **AVERAGE** · · · · · Work is the basis for my identity

We are people who tend toward idolatry. We create idols and build our lives around them. For many, the body and how it looks is an idol. For some, wealth and possessions are idols. For numerous mothers, the calling to be a mother becomes an idol. And for many, whether they realize it or not, work is an idol. When something becomes everything to us, that is idolatry.

Let's consider work again but this time from God's perspective. Our work is meant to be an expression of who we are as God's handiwork. Because of who God is and how he sees us, as evidenced in the gift of his Son, Jesus Christ, we must be worth something. We have value, worth, dignity, and adequacy, because God has declared that we have them. Instead of our work giving us a sense of value, worth, dignity, and adequacy as Christians, it is the other way around.

The *way* we do our job is an expression of the high value God has ascribed in us.

The *proficiency* of the level of our work is an expression of the high value God has ascribed to us.

We bring *dignity* to our work because God has given us a sense of dignity. As believers, we have the opportunity to do a job out of the sense of *adequacy* we have because of God's declaration that we are adequate. We should not work to make us feel adequate. If we search the Scriptures, we discover that we are special and worthwhile only because of God.

What would happen to you and the quality of your work if your attitude was this: *My work is an expression of me and the presence of God in my life!* It would be the beginning of feeling good about yourself, in spite of what may be going on at your job.

Work is also a source for at least some of our social life. Here is where we meet people, make lasting friendships, and have social interaction. Our job helps us network with others, and the socialization occurs even during working hours. But what happens when the job is no longer there? Do you take your friends with you? Do you have as much contact with them as when you worked together? Do they call you, or are you the one who has to stay in touch with them most of the time? If your identity is tied into these social relationships, how do you feel about yourself when this source dries up? Let me give you an example.

John had spent more than two decades as a crossing guard. He was loved by scores of children and parents alike. In fact, during the last two years on the job, he had begun to cross the young children of some of the children he had helped cross years before. But eventually, he found he could no longer carry out his duties.

"I miss those kids," he said. "I didn't have that much contact with many other folks, but twice a day I saw those kids, talked with them, and got to know their folks. Even when I wasn't on duty during Christmas vacation. I would receive cards and gifts from them. Those kids were my whole life. It gave me the friends and grandkids I never had. Now it's really lonely not getting to that corner each day."

What about you? To what extent do you base your identity on the social relationships and connections you have through your job? Evaluate yourself, using the scale of 0 to 10:

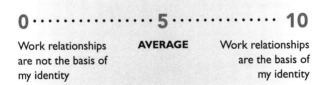

0 · · · · · · · · · · · · · 5 · · · · · · · · · · · · 10

| Work relationships are not the basis of my identity | **AVERAGE** | Work relationships are the basis of my identity |

Work is also used as a source of status and prestige. The name of the firm, the size of our cubbyhole or office, how close the office is to the president, whether or not we have a secretary, our title, whether or not we are given a company car (and the kind of car!)—all of these factors are tied into status and prestige.

However, with a changing economy, ongoing wars and the ever-present threat of new wars, and inroads from foreign distributors and companies, no profession or job is absolutely secure. All it would take is a small recession and the company car would be recalled, the office would vanish, the sales territory would be reshaped, and a new nebulous title has little or no meaning would be bestowed. Then how would you feel about yourself? Such losses can be devastating, especially if other people know about all that you have lost at work. The loss of face is an added blow.

Using the scale of 0 to 10, evaluate to what extent work is your source of status and prestige:

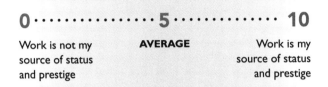

0 · · · · · · · · · · · · · 5 · · · · · · · · · · · · 10

Work is not my   **AVERAGE**   Work is my
source of status   source of status
and prestige   and prestige

Work has another meaning for most people. It is an opportunity for self-expression. You can achieve, be creative, and perhaps have some new experiences. For those who feel this way about their work, retirement is seen as an enemy rather than something to be anticipated. As one man said, "When I had to retire, I dried up. I stagnated. My avenue for expression was taken away."

Is work your source of expressing who you are? If so, what will happen when you retire? Take time now to evaluate whether work is your basis for expressing your identity:

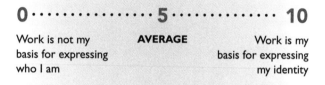

0 · · · · · · · · · · · · · · 5 · · · · · · · · · · · · 10

Work is not my
basis for expressing
who I am

AVERAGE

Work is my
basis for expressing
my identity

For a number of people, work is an opportunity to serve others. It is easy to think of a number of occupations that have serving as their basic purpose. But service can be part of most occupations, because serving is really based on the attitude or motivation of the person. For some, serving others is life's calling, and they seek a profession that affords them that opportunity. But when they retire and their outlet is cut off, how do they handle this loss? For some, it is devastating. For others, it isn't a problem. Why? What makes the difference?

Evaluate your own thoughts about the extent your work is an expression of serving others:

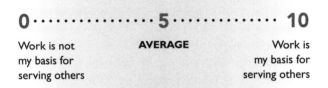

0	5	10
Work is not my basis for serving others	**AVERAGE**	Work is my basis for serving others

Finally, for a large number of people, work is simply an opportunity to fill time. It is their way of taking care of the mundane, humdrum part of life. Take away the job and they become bored. Some occupations do tend to lend themselves to this work attitude. But even if work means only this, what happens when that mandatory retirement age is reached or illness necessitates leaving the job. Then the time filler is lost.

Is your work a time filler? Evaluate whether work is a time filler for you:

0 · · · · · · · · · · · · · · **5** · · · · · · · · · · · · **10**

Work is not the way I fill time   **AVERAGE**   Work is the way I fill time

Now reflect on all the ways work can be the foundation of your identity. What do your answers tell you about work as a source of your identity?

0 · · · · · · · · · · · · · · **5** · · · · · · · · · · · · **10**

Work is not the source of my identity   **AVERAGE**   Work is the source of my identity

Your Identity during the Family Life Cycle

The empty-nest stage of the family life cycle is an interesting adjustment. For some couples, the empty nest signifies a major loss. It can actually be a mingling of numerous feelings as expressed in Ecclesiastes 3:1–8: a time of weeping, laughing, mourning, healing, loving, releasing, losing, and relief. The atmosphere of the home changes. There are fewer choices to make, less confusion and noise. Patterns of shopping, cooking, and scheduling change.

I have several relatives who raise large families on their farms. The mothers are used to cooking large meals for their brood, but the day will come when that role will no longer need to be filled. New roles will have to be established, and often, new pressures will be felt. Needs formerly filled by children will be diverted to others for fulfillment.

Sometimes an additional loss occurs if the couple lunges toward each other to fill the empty spaces in their lives. They may end up pushing each other away because of their intensity, and a feeling of abandonment can result. If a couple has relied on their children to hold their relationship together or to give them something to focus on, the departure of the last child creates an enormous loss within the marital relationship as well.

The mother who has relied on that role as the primary source of her identity may end up feeling abandoned, unloved, uncared for, and depressed, because her identity has been removed. If she gave up a career to have children, the departure of the last child can even elicit resentment. It could also bring to light the fact that intimacy has been absent in the marriage for many years, for the camouflage is no longer there. A working mother, however, often has an easier time adjusting, because she already has another outlet that helps her cope with her loss.

The empty nest affects fathers also. A child who was Mother's little girl at six may have become Dad's special pal. When she leaves, he could feel devastated. The departure of a child points out to him that life could be passing him by faster than he likes.

Your Identity at Midlife: Men and Women

All men go through a midlife transition that has the potential for growth, new direction, and new life. It is all right to evaluate, question, and ultimately discover a new sense of purpose. But the man who for years has sold his identity to the pursuit of a dream through his vocation may hit a brick wall when he reaches the middle years of his life. Sometime in midlife, he realizes that he is never really going to attain his goal and fulfill his dream. Or maybe he has arrived at his goal and says to himself, *So what? There's got to be more than this. Is this all?* A sense of loss and emptiness sets in. The man who has lived a solitary life without close male friends has never learned to experience or express his feelings; and having built his identity on his work, he is the one who is most prone to experience this classic male midlife crisis.

There are many women today who build identity through performance, appearance, or motherhood. They too come to a midlife place where they feel,

Is this all there is? Or they are confronted with diminishing performances and appearance, or the children leave home. Unfortunately, more attention has been given to men's midlife transitions than to those of women, which may mean less help or understanding is available for women.

YOUR DREAMS

The substance of life is made up of dreams and desires. We need them. Our society needs them. It is out of dreams that motivations are born, new inventions and approaches come about, and people feel a purpose. That is why the death of a dream can be so devastating.

We seem to feel that most dreams come from those who are young. Remember what your dreams were when you were young? Perhaps they had to do with your vocation or with the amount of money you were going to make. Maybe your dream was about something you would create. For example, I always wanted to live where I could experience a forest and the seasons.

Finally, at the age of fifty, a portion of that dream came true, but not in the way that I had dreamed.

What about your dreams? Which ones have come true? Which did you give up? What are your dreams at the present time?

_____

_____

_____

_____

_____

In high school I had friends who dreamed of what they were going to achieve. As I reflect on some of my dreams and theirs and on the dreams I often hear about in my counseling office, I realize there were two categories of dreams: realistic and unrealistic.

Some of them are attainable. Others are mere fantasies that will never make it in the real world. The young, aspiring actress who sees acting as giving her identity and meaning in life may discover the road to success in her profession may include shallowness, manipulation, and conniving; and her dream may be destroyed. The Peace Corps worker who dreams of changing the future of a small tribe may come to realize that he or she will not be the one to make that happen. And so often I hear about a wife's dream of having a happy fulfilled marriage and how that dream crumbled when her partner walked out the door.

The older we become, the less we dream, since we have less energy, time, and even desire. Letting go of some of the dreams we had as young people is part of becoming realistic adults. Judith Viorst talks about "necessary losses" in her book of that title. We need to experience some losses to move into the next phase of life.[2]

It is easy to give up a dream? Not really. Dreams give us hope and inspiration. They may not be as visual as having a car totaled in an accident, but they are just as real to us.

Have you ever thought about how your identity is tied into your dreams? Take away your dreams, and who are you? How do lost dreams affect how you feel about yourself? Giving up a dream calls you to experience the reality, not only that do you not have

> Growing older doesn't have to mean the death of our dreams.

the ability or time to achieve this dream, but also that someday you won't even be here! There is an ending to this earthly life.

Not all of our dreams have to be profound. I grew up with music. I played piano, clarinet, and saxophone. I had many enjoyable experiences in bands and orchestras, but I always wanted to play the trumpet. It was a dream and a desire of mine, especially when I heard some of the greats.

One day when I was about forty-eight, I was thinking about my wish to play the trumpet. Then I thought, *Well, what's keeping you from playing?* And I responded, *Nothing.* So I found a teacher, rented a trumpet (and eventually purchased one), and for a few years I took lessons. Then I stopped, for several reasons. I had learned enough to play some tunes (in key), and that was fulfilling. In fact it was a real boost to me when the dogs quit leaving the room when I practiced. But in addition to my feeling fulfilled, the reality of what I wanted to do hit me as well. At my age, my lip muscles were not going to respond as well as they would have if I had started learning to play the trumpet when I was a child. I didn't have the amount of time to put in each day to achieve the level I had once dreamed of when I was younger. Putting all of that together helped me make the decision to stop. I had realized a dream, although not to the extent that I had originally hoped. This is a process that all of us have to face in many areas of our lives as we become older.

But growing older doesn't have to mean the death of our dreams. They can be revised, reshaped and refashioned to meet the reality of who and what we are, as well as the reality of our abilities. I have met people in their fifties, sixties, and seventies who still had dreams. These people are survivors.[3]

Your Self-Esteem

One of the most frequently asked questions of counselors, especially by women, has to do with identity and self-esteem based on what other people have said. All ages struggle with this issue, and in spite of all the teaching and resources available for help, the conflict still continues.

Basing our identity on what others say about us is the same as building on a false foundation. One such example of this is believing what others have said about us in the past. A child hears her parents say, "She never cleans her room," or she hears teachers say, "You're just one of those slow learners." So she grows up believing she is a sloppy, homely, stupid girl. Her identity is based on the comments of others. Did that happen to you? Those comments may not be true, but if you believed them, they *became* true for you and you have acted them out as your identity.

If you have based your identity on what others have said about you, you have given those people tremendous power and control over your life. But are you sure their perceptions were accurate? Are there other people who can give you a more accurate picture of who you really are? How does the perception of you by other people compare to God's perception?

_____

_____

_____

_____

_____

_____

_____

_____

_____

_____

YOUR SOCIAL STATUS

There are four main standards that society has that many people mistakenly use as a basis for their identity.

1. *Accomplishments.* Some people base their identity on what they accomplish and how they perform. They believe that what they do earns them a certain status rating, which can increase based on the kinds of tasks or roles in which they become involved. Do you?

2. *Possessions.* Some base their identity on what they possess or own. They have an insatiable need to acquire things. When they do not feel good about themselves, they head for the mall or go shopping on the Internet. They struggle with the tendency to compare their possessions to what other people have. Do you?

3. *Who They Know.* Still others base their identity on who they know. Unfortunately, these people end up being name-droppers who tend to be threatened by the status of others, or people who become a threat to others in their quest for status. Do you?

4. *Appearance.* Many base their identity on how they feel about their appearance. This applies especially to women. They spend countless hours in front of the mirror. They change clothes several times a day and spend an excessive amount of money on beauty aids. Their entire day or evening can be ruined if they feel unattractive. I emphasize a woman's feelings about herself, because her attractiveness is largely based on her perception of how she looks. Although her perceptions are often based on the reactions of others, if a woman doesn't see herself as attractive, the compliments of others have no effect—even if twenty-five people rave about her appearance. Are you like this?

I like what one author has said about these false foundations:

> When we contrast our appearance, our accomplishments, our friends or our possessions to others we are making a comparison based in large part on fantasy. Perhaps this is one of the reasons why soap operas and romance novels are so popular today.
>
> When we believe we are only worthwhile if we are beautiful, if we use the right products, if we know the right people, if we are successful, or if we are financially comfortable, we are building our self-image on faulty foundations.
>
> When we swallow these faddish opinions, society loves us because we fit its mold. But what happens when the mold changes?[4]

I've talked with numerous men and women who have built their identity on one or more of these tenuous foundations.

YOUR BELIEFS ABOUT YOURSELF

What do you believe about yourself? Is your identity based on a faulty foundation? Perhaps these questions will help you know where you are at this time in your life.

1. Do you believe that there is something inherently wrong or bad about you?

   _____

   _____

2. Do you believe your adequacy is defined by the approval or disapproval of others? If so, who are these people? Did your mother or father disapprove of you? If so, how does that make you feel?

   _____

   _____

   _____

3. Do you believe your adequacy is tied to how much money you make? Where did this belief originate?

_____

_____

_____

4. Do you believe that you always must be right about everything to be adequate or feel good about yourself? Do you believe that if you are wrong, you will be disapproved of or rejected?

_____

_____

_____

5. Do you believe that you're inadequate because you are overly sensitive?

_____

_____

6. Do you believe that you're helpless and powerless?

_____

_____

7. Do you believe that you must please everyone in order to be worthwhile?

_____

_____

8. Do you believe that your adequacy is tied to how much education you've had?

_____

_____

9. Do you believe that your adequacy and worth are tied to how you look? How tall or short you are? How fat or thin you are?[5]

_____

_____

Most of us have residing within us a critic that significantly influences what we believe about ourselves and how we respond to others. Your internal critic is like a condemning conscience. It operates on the basis of standards that were developed in response to the judgments and evaluations of your parents and other people you looked up to. Your internal critic is quick to point out that you do not measure up to these standards.

YOUR PAST

Are you limited by your past? Have you ever felt as if life would be a lot easier if only those wounds and negative experiences from the past didn't keep interfering? Have you ever felt that way when you wake up in the morning? You just can't get going? I've heard people say, "I really want to move ahead with my life. I'm committed to it, but it's so hard to get going." You don't like the identity you have, but you can't seem to rebuild.

I understand that. Sometimes hurts and issues from the past slow us down. You have to keep trying hard and expending so much effort before you finally start moving ahead. Excess emotional baggage can bog you down and rob you of blessing.

As a counselor for more than forty years, I have talked with hundreds of people who are struggling with the effects of their past. Some of them are able to break free and move forward with their lives. Some cannot. Some struggle so hard just to make a slight bit of progress. Many are depressed because of what happened to them or because so many years were wasted before they finally came for counseling. I see it in their identity.

I've found that people deal with their emotional baggage in several inappropriate ways. Many of them are riddled with r*egret over missed opportunities*. I often hear people say things like, "If only I had..." and "Oh, how I regret..." Another way we live our lives in the past is described by Jack Hayford as "the remembrance of reversals." [6] Reversals are similar to regrets except that this time the focus is on what might have been—"if only that hadn't happened" and "if only I could have done it differently." Sometimes to expedite the process of growth and change, I ask counselees to make me a list of all their "if onlys" and regrets, so we can tackle each of them and eventually put them to rest.

But many of the regrets I hear about are vain regrets. Whether we regret what was done to us by others or what we have done to others (sins), our looking back to the past only cripples the blessings of the present and detours us from entering the future. I'm not saying that we should never regret the past. There is a place and time for this—once! And then we must begin moving in a new direction.

> You can get unstuck from the quicksand of past hurts by choosing to let God work in your life today.

We all have baggage and personal failures from the past. The past is past, and the events in that time frame can never be changed. But the effects can.

John was a middle-aged man who had been in counseling for some time. He had experienced a number of difficulties growing up, and the effects had stayed with him. From time to time his unresolved problems from the past erupted and this, in turn, led to disruptions in his family and work life. In counseling he tended to rehearse over and over what had happened to him and his poor choices at a younger age. The best way to put it is that he was bemoaning the past.

"John," I said, 'it sounds like you really regret what has happened in the past. It also sounds like you feel that some of your life has been wasted because of the past. If that is so, wouldn't it be best now to focus your time and energy on moving on from what happened by making your present life different? I know the past can't be changed, but the present and future can.

"John, because you're a Christian and you don't have to live your life by yourself, why not let God restore those lost years by what he can do and help what you can do in the present? God is asking you to give him the past and rejoice in who you are right at this moment because of him. I think he has some surprises in store for you. What about it, John?"

What about you? You can get unstuck from the quicksand of past hurts by choosing to let God work in your life today.

Another dangerous tactic we use in handling the past is *recrimination*. We attempt to make others atone for what they did to us in the past. Blame and recrimination bring us to resentment, which leads to a lack of forgiveness; and we end up with a festering, painful memory.

Another common response to the past is *renunciation*. We promise to change and do things differently. Past behaviors and attitudes are simply renounced, but they are not confronted and cleansed. Dr. Lloyd Ogilvie puts this so well when he says:

> We try to close the door on what has been, but all we do is suppress the dragons of memory. Every so often they rap persistently and want to come out into our consciousness for a dress rehearsal in preparation for a rerun in a new situation or circumstance. Renunciation of our memories

sounds so very pious. The only thing wrong with it is that it doesn't work.[7]

Instead of dragging along the unnecessary baggage of regret, blame, and renunciation, have you ever tried rejoicing over the past? That may sound strange, but rejoicing eventually brings release. Rejoicing over the past doesn't mean that you deny the hurtful incidents or the pain they brought you. Rather you come to the place where you no longer ask why but how: How can I learn from what happened to me and be a different person because of it?

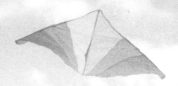

CHAPTER THREE

Letting Go of
Your False Identity

Why cling any longer to your false identity when God has called you to something better? Consider God's alternatives for your faulty beliefs about yourself and discover how to appropriate them.

I have talked with many who say, "I really want to get rid of some of my old beliefs about myself. They do nothing but limit me. I really think it's time to clean house."

I usually answer, "That's a good beginning, but what about the rest of the work?"

"What other work?" they ask.

"Housecleaning is only half of the job," I answer. "You also need to redecorate. Some of your deeply entrenched beliefs may not be that easy to dispose of. You will need to replace them with new, accurate, and positive beliefs about yourself.

CLEANING OUT NEGATIVE THOUGHTS

The Bible warns that housecleaning is a process we must take seriously. Consider Matthew 12:43-45:

> When an impure spirit comes out of a person, it goes through arid places seeking rest and does not find it. Then it says, "I will return to the house I left." When it arrives, it finds the house unoccupied, swept clean and put in order. Then it goes and takes with it seven other spirits more wicked than itself, and they go in and live there. And the final condition of that person is worse than the first. That is how it will be with this wicked generation.

Think about the place where you have all of your thoughts as your house. It's furnished throughout with everything you think about yourself and the world. It also includes many "furnishings" that were handed down to you by others.

These furnishings include the toxic or negative self-talk you inherited from parents, friends, siblings, teachers, and others. These individuals gave you your furnishings, and you've held on to them for years, continuing to use them. Some of this tattered, hand-me-down furniture sags with wear and threatens to collapse.

Now, suppose a friend has agreed to help you get rid of the junk. He's going to help you eliminate negative thinking patterns permanently. They'll be gone for good. So the two of you meet and begin boxing everything up, carrying every single item out of the house and into the garage. Rugs, stove, beds, tables, chairs—everything's on its way out. Every old self-belief now is stored in the garage, where no one can see it.

When your friend leaves, you go back inside the house. It looks so much larger without any of the furnishings. It's empty. It's clean. It smells better. There's not one negative thought available anywhere. You begin to think, *Now I'll have positive thoughts! I'll be a positive thinker!*

There you are—alone with your big, empty house. You wander from room to room. You like it, now that you've removed all those old, worn negative thoughts.

But your house feels so empty. An hour goes by. Two. Three.

You're thinking, *This is great! I've evicted all my old negative thoughts. There's not one in sight!*

But the emptiness gets to you. So after a while, you decide to revisit the old stuff. You go out to the garage. You see an item that feels so familiar. It's this old negative thought: *I don't have much to offer in a relationship.*

You think, *This won't hurt anything. I'll just take this one item back.*

A bit later, you repeat the process. And over the next few hours, you retrieve all of the junk. Why? Because you're comfortable with all those thoughts, bad as they are. You're used to them.

FILLING YOUR MIND WITH POSITIVE THOUGHTS

We have difficulty with a void or vacuum in our mind. If we simply try to empty our mind of negative thoughts but fail to replace them with positive thoughts, the negative thoughts will return.

When you clean out your house, it's more productive to discard or destroy the old furniture, rather than store it, keeping it available. You'll be more successful bringing in a load of new furniture—positive thoughts about yourself that reflect God's view of you and your true identity.

Keep this in mind and remind yourself of this each day: You are a *created* image bearer. That's right—you bear the image of God and *he* chose to create you this way. This is who you are, and this is the basis for your identity. (It also helps to remind yourself that the members of your

> You are a created image bearer.

family and everyone else you know were created in the image of God as well!)

> Then God said, "*Let us make mankind in our image, in our likeness, so that they may rule over the fish in the sea and the birds in the sky, over the livestock and all the wild animals, and over all the creatures that move along the ground.*"
>
> — Genesis 1:26

REFLECTING GOD IN WHO YOU ARE

God made us to reflect him just as a mirror reflects an image. When you look at yourself in a mirror, remember you're looking at the image of God.

God didn't make anything else in his image. It's as though God honored us by choosing us for this purpose. How quickly we forget this. We allow other things to get in the way of us remembering that we're made in his image. Whether we realize it or not, it's as though we choose other factors to build our identity upon and we hang onto them as though they were an idol. But perhaps we do and are ignorant about its existence.

Earlier in the book we talked about four main standards that people use as a basis for their identity: accomplishments, possessions, other people or "who you know," and appearance. Many people build their image on these false foundations and forget, "I'm made in the image of God—that's who I am. None of the above compare." Remind yourself daily, "I'm made in the image of God and I'm called to reflect his glory."

BUILDING YOUR NEW IDENTITY

It's important that you let go of your past identity (based on inaccurate messages about you) and that you build a new identity based on the unconditional love and acceptance of God. To do so, you need unconditional love and your true, God-given identity. Once you decide which identity is of greater value, then you need to let go of one and grab for the other.

Dr. Paul Tournier compares Christian growth to the experience of swinging from a trapeze. The man on the trapeze clings to the bar because it is his security. When another trapeze bar swings into view, he needs to release his grip on one bar in order to leap to the other. It's a scary process. Similarly, God is swinging a new trapeze bar into your view. It is a positive, accurate, new identity based on God's Word. But in order to grasp the new, you have got to release the old. You may have difficulty relinquishing the familiarity and security of your old identity. But think of what you will gain.[8]

BEING AMAZED BY GRACE[9]

There is a word that is foundational for our life identity as Christians. It's actually life changing. "Grace." You may be curious about or wondering what grace is. Throughout the Bible the word "grace" is used in relation to *favor*, particularly divine favor or help that is not earned but bestowed as a gift. Philip Yancey defines grace this way in his book *What's So Amazing About Grace?*

> Grace makes its appearance in so many forms that I have trouble defining it. I am ready, I thought, to attempt something like a definition of grace in relation to God. *Grace means there is nothing we can do to make God love us more*—no amount of spiritual calisthenics and renunciations, no amount of knowledge gained from seminaries and divinity schools, no amount of crusading on behalf of righteous causes. *And grace means there is nothing we can do to make God love us less*—no amount of racism or pride or pornography or adultery or even

murder. Grace means that God already loves us as much as an infinite God can possibly love.[10]

You and I are like a bank account that has insufficient funds. We're always in debt. And we end up in despair. But if we're walking with Christ, we have been saved by grace and are made alive by grace. John Ortberg, in *Love Beyond Reason*, gives a clear description of what God's grace has done:

> This is grace for anyone who's ever despaired over sin. This is the removal of our mountain of moral indebtedness. If you've ever felt that gap between reality and who you're called to be, ever felt like you can't close it—this is grace for you. God took our indebtedness and guilt and nailed it to the cross. He erased the bill, destroyed the IOU, so you are free. Unburdened. Cleansed. You can live with a heart as light as a feather. Today—no matter what you did yesterday. This is the wonder of grace.[11]

The Price of Grace

Grace is totally free. It cannot be bought. It is undeserved, unearned, and cannot be repaid. Ephesians 2:4-5 says, "But because of his great love for us, God, who is rich in mercy, made us alive with Christ even when we were dead in transgressions—it is by grace you have been saved."

God doesn't say . . .

"I love you because . . ."

"I love you since . . ."

"I will love you if . . ."

"I will love you when . . ."

"I will love you after . . ."

"I will love you provided . . ."

In no way is God's love conditional.[12]

Simply put, grace extends favor and kindness to one who doesn't deserve it and can never earn it. Every time you think of the word "grace," think undeserved, undeserved, undeserved.

During the Napoleonic Wars, a young, battle-weary French soldier fell asleep while on guard duty. He was court-martialed, found guilty, and sentenced to death. His widowed mother somehow arranged an audience with Emperor Napoleon himself. Falling prostrate at the emperor's feet, she begged for her son's life to be spared, explaining he was her only child and her sole means of support. Napoleon grew weary of her pleas. "Madam, your son does not deserve mercy. He deserves to die," he said coldly. To which the mother immediately replied, "Of course, sire, you are right. That's why I am asking you to show mercy on him. If he were deserving, it wouldn't be mercy." Napoleon was so touched by the logic of her statement that he pardoned the soldier.

If we were deserving, it wouldn't be grace. It is undeserved and unmerited. It is God's free gift, completely unobstructed by our sin, our guilt, and our unworthiness.

Grace is given free and clear with no strings attached.

The Transforming Power of Grace

Grace can simply be defined as a free gift from God that results in giving you significance and value at a new level. Grace is God's kind disposition, unconditional love, concern, compassion, and favor toward you, no matter the circumstance—yes, no matter the situation. The greatest gift of his grace was given to us through Christ.

> Because of Christ's redemption,
>
> I am a new creation of infinite worth.
>
> I am deeply loved,
>
> I am completely forgiven,
>
> I am totally pleasing,
>
> I am totally accepted by God,
>
> I am absolutely complete in Christ.
>
> When my performance
>
> Reflects my new identity in Christ,
>
> That reflection is dynamically unique.
>
> There has never been another person like me
>
> In the history of mankind,
>
> Nor will there ever be.

God has made me an original,

One of a kind,

A special person.[13]

Read these statements out loud each day for a week and discover the difference these true statements will make in your life and how you will see yourself. You will indeed have a new identity.

You have been declared someone special—and you are! As it says in Ephesians 1:4-5:

Long ago, even before he made the world, God chose us to be his very own through what Christ would do for us; he decided then to make us holy in his eyes, without a single fault—we who stand before him covered with his love. His unchanging plan has always been to adopt us into his own family by sending Jesus Christ to die for us. And he did this because he wanted to! (TLB).

Another Bible version gives as the last phrase: "It gave him great pleasure" (NLT).

Yet as beautiful as these words are, they are so hard for most of us to grasp and truly believe about ourselves. Once we are in God's grace, however—once we receive and embrace it—grace begins to transform us. God himself uses it to heal us of every sin, every sense of inadequacy, every bit of pain from our past. This is *healing* grace. Don't let grace slip past you any longer; *experience* it. God wants you to experience it! And not only as a one-time emotional event but as a *lifestyle*, as something you breathe and live and *give out*.

We become people of grace when we give out what we've been given. Focusing on someone other than yourself is sometimes the first step in getting over the pain of depression, loneliness and despair. Whatever you focus on will increase in your heart and mind. The point is that the focus on self leads to many heartaches and defeats. If you're tired of focusing on your failures and on the ways that others have failed you, then healing grace is for you. It is for you to freely receive and to freely give.

The Practice of Grace

Grace has a number of phrases that can change your relationship with others. Here are six of them:

1. "I was wrong."

2. "You were right."

3. "I am sorry."

4. "I forgive you."

5. "Please forgive me."

6. "I love you."

Carefully read these phrases, and then take a minute to write them down on a 3x5 card or on your smart phone or tablet to keep with you. Put the list somewhere where you'll see it frequently. We hope these phrases will begin to enhance your vocabulary. Over time these phrases will become second nature to you, easily spoken in moments of need. As Proverbs 25:11 says, may these words be "like apples of gold in settings of silver."

Do you think you could use these words the next time you encounter conflict with someone who rubs you the wrong way? What about when you think of a parent, spouse, or significant other who abused or neglected you? Perhaps that seems impossible now, but in time, with the grace of God and a willingness in your heart to change, you will be able to speak these words and communicate grace to even your worst offenders. You will feel differently.

The Healing Power of Grace

Some of us struggle with who we are because we have made bad choices and we have a hard time admitting them.

Not all people are victims of their own choices. Some are clearly victims of the abuses and errors or sins of others, particularly of those close to them.

The message you need to hear is that you can go forward to receive the abundant life God has for you. God's healing grace is sufficient for your cure (see 2 Corinthians 12:9). You may need to make major changes in how you think about yourself and the Lord's love for you. Or you may just need to receive his gift of grace. But you do not have to remain a victim.

Healing grace enables us to move away from being victims of others' actions to being conquerors in Christ. By the power of the Holy Spirit and the transforming work of God's Word, we can get out of patterns of negative self-talk and into a mindset based on grace. We can let go of self-hatred and learn how to love and forgive ourselves and others because Christ unconditionally loves us.

We can break free from blaming others for our issues and from the bondage of unforgiveness. It is not God's will for us to wallow in resentment any longer.

"Healing grace" isn't simply a magical phrase or philosophy that we subscribe to as another self-help tool.

The premise to *healing grace* is that Jesus Christ has to rule in a person's heart in order for true healing to take place. When Christ is the center of your life, grace freely flows from him to you and through Christ in you to others. He becomes for you the source of living water and the bread of life. Jesus becomes the center of your universe. When processed through him, the problems you have become smaller, easier to solve, and less of a threat to your existence and your personal worth.

Jesus says, "Follow me. I am. I will. Fear not. Just believe" (see Matthew 4:19; 16:24; 19:21; John 10:27; Isaiah 41:10; 46:9; 55:11; Joshua 1:9) and "You can!" (see Mark 9:23). The results of letting Jesus be in charge of your life are amazing.

In *Deadly Emotions*, Dr. Don Colbert tells about a man in the seventeenth century who discovered a fascinating principle. Dutch mathematician, astronomer, and physicist Christian Huygens invented the pendulum clock and began manufacturing pendulum clocks to sell. One evening he was lying in bed and noticed that all of the pendulums were swinging in unison, even though he knew for sure they hadn't started out that way. So he got out of bed and restarted them, purposefully setting them at different times to break the synchronized rhythm. In a brief period of time they began swinging together again. Years later scientists discovered that the largest clock with the strongest rhythm pulled the other pendulums into sync with itself. The strongest biological oscillator in our body is our heart, and it acts like the largest pendulum clock. It has the ability to pull every other bodily system into its own rhythm. When your heart is at peace, as ruled by Christ, all the rest of your body experiences the influence of his presence. But if self is at the center, your life is out of sync.[14]

Jesus says, "Follow me. I am. I will. Fear not. Just believe. You can!"

Spiritually speaking, when Jesus is at the center of your life or heart, his presence, his peace, is communicated to every aspect of your life, such as your body, your mind, and your relationships. When Jesus is at the center, you will be amazed at the difference![15] And when Jesus is the center of your life, what you do and say will reflect his grace, which is God's gift of unconditional love and forgiveness to us though Jesus Christ. Your grace-filled life will be one that is healed and is helping others heal through the gift of grace.

Belonging to God

The bottom line is this: we don't belong to ourselves; we belong to God. Let's consider this in a different way.

In order to truly appreciate that we belong to God, that he loves us unconditionally in Christ, and that he smiles on us daily, we need to gain a deeper understanding of who we are and what we are becoming as his children. Let's consider several sections from Ephesians 1 that describe our identity in God's family.

We have already talked about the good news in Ephesians 1:3-4—that God has blessed us eternally in Christ by choosing us to be his. Verses 4-5 tell us how close our relationship with God is: "In love he predestined us for adoption to sonship through Jesus Christ." You're not a stranger to God. You're not even a distant relative. God has chosen you to be his child. You are blessed!

Imagine that you are standing outside your church one Sunday morning after the service and a visitor approaches you and says, "By the way, did you know that you and I came from the same adoption agency? When were you adopted?"

Now I can imagine a number of ways you might respond to this person. One response would be surprise as you wonder which planet this stranger just flew in from. You might even say, "I don't know what you're talking about. I wasn't adopted. I grew up with my natural parents, and they're still living. And you and I certainly didn't come from the same family."

The stranger replies, "But it's true. We are from the same adopted family. When were you adopted?"

In reality, both of you are correct, but you're talking about two different experiences. If you both know Jesus Christ as Savior, you were both adopted into God's family. The apostle John wrote: "To all who did receive him, to those who believed in his name, he gave the right to become children of God" (John 1:12). Romans 8:16 states: "The Spirit himself testifies with our spirit that we are God's children." Understanding the fullness of your spiritual adoption can redirect your thinking and response to life. Your adoption is a gift of grace. This is how you have been chosen for blessing.

In Roman law during New Testament times, it was common practice for a childless adult who wanted an heir to adopt an adult male as his son. We too have been adopted by God as his heirs.[16] The apostle Paul wrote: "Now if we are children, then we are heirs—heirs of God and co-heirs with Christ" (Romans 8:17); "So you are no longer a slave, but God's child, God has made also an heir" (Galatians 4:7).

What are some of the rights and privileges you inherited? Ephesians lists many of them:

> ➤ You have been guaranteed eternal life, as evidenced by the presence of the Holy Spirit in your life (see 1:13-14).

> ➤ You have hope in Christ, your "glorious inheritance" (1:18).

> ➤ You have experienced the incomparable power that raised Jesus Christ from the dead and seated him at God's right hand (see 1:19-20).

➤ You are the recipient of God's incomparable grace that saved you apart from anything you have done or will ever do (see 2:8-9).

➤ You now have access to the Father through his Spirit (see 2:18).

➤ You can know the love of Christ, which will enable you to receive God's fullness (see 3:19).

I have worked with a number of clients who were physically adopted as children. They have shared with me how they felt when they first learned that they had been adopted. Some had been delighted to know that someone cared enough about them to select them. But others had been angry and resentful toward their natural parents for abandoning them. Some had been upset at both sets of parents.

How do you feel about being adopted by the King of the universe and being delivered from the kingdom of darkness (see Colossians 1:13)? This is one of the greatest blessings that the gospel offers you. You have been taken into God's family and fellowship, and you have been established as his child and heir. You may have come from a dysfunctional home and perhaps experienced emotional or physical abuse in your natural family. But God is the Father who can fill the gaps in your life. Because you are in a family, closeness, affection, and generosity are the basis of your relationship with your Father God. Your relationship as an heir is the basis for your Christian life and the foundation for all of the other blessings you receive in your day-to-day experience.

Our relationship as adopted children of God has a number of implications for the way we live our lives. Just as a child grows up imitating his or her father and mother, so we can become more and more like our Father God.

We are told how to do this, for example, in the Sermon on the Mount in which Christ calls us to *imitate* our Father: "Love your enemies and pray for those who persecute you. Be perfect, therefore, as your heavenly Father is perfect" (Matthew 5:44,48).

We are also called to *glorify* our Father: "Let your light shine before others, that they may see your good deeds and glorify your Father in heaven" (Matthew 5:16).

We are called to *please* our Father: "When you give to the needy, do not let your left hand know what your right hand is doing, so that your giving may be in secret. Then your Father, who sees what is done in secret, will reward you. . . . When you pray, go into your room, close the door and pray to your Father, who is unseen. Then your Father, who sees what is done in secret, will reward you" (Matthew 6:3-6).

As we imitate, glorify and please our Father, we begin to sense the thrill of participating in the destiny for which we were created. We not only enjoy the blessing of *being* God's children, but we also realize the personal benefits that come from *behaving* as God's

> God spared nothing to secure for you an eternal identity in Christ.

children. Our knowledge of God grows, as does our awareness of his knowledge and love for us. As we live out our identity as God's adopted children, day by day, we are personally transformed. We are blessed with the understanding that we are fulfilling our purpose in life.

Not only is our blessing based on being chosen and adopted by God, but also when we are asked who we are, we are blessed by being able to reply, "I am a forgiven person." The death of Jesus Christ was the complete payment for everything you have done wrong: "In him we have redemption through his blood, the forgiveness of sins, in accordance with the riches of God's grace. When you believed, you were marked in him with a seal, the promised Holy Spirit, who is a deposit guaranteeing our inheritance" (Ephesians 1:7,13-14).

It's not that God decided just to excuse our sins and say, "No problem. I'll just dismiss the charges." No. The penalty for our sins had to be paid. God spared nothing to secure for you an eternal identity in Christ. He willingly gave his cherished Son in order give you the right to be with him forever. Not only that, you are safe in his care forever.

Perhaps the best way to explain the security we

enjoy is to describe how I feel when I go to my bank and ask to see my safety deposit box. I have to sign in to prove my ownership, have my signature evaluated, and have to produce the proper key. Only then will the attendant take out the bank's key and use both keys to let me see my box.

When I leave, my box is locked up and the outer doors of the safe are locked as well. I go away feeling comfortable and confident that my valuables are well protected. I rest assured that they will always be there whenever I need them.

Of course, my sense of security is based on human standards and structures. Unfortunately, human measures of security have their limitations. Even the most securely guarded banks and locked vaults can be robbed.

But there is a spiritual security we share that has no limitations. In Ephesians 1:13 there is a word that we don't usually use: "seal." To the readers of Paul's day, the term was significant. At that time in history, the seal of Rome signified ownership and security and was the ultimate sign of surety. People relied upon it for security and authority. The tomb of Jesus was sealed (see Matthew 27:65-66). Unfortunately, the seal of the Roman Empire wasn't indestructible. It could be broken, just like my safety deposit box can be broken into by some clever criminal.

But you and I have been *sealed* by the Holy Spirit, and we are totally secure in Jesus Christ. We have been purchased by the blood of Christ. God owns me, and if you have surrendered your life to Jesus Christ, then God owns you. You don't have to be concerned about being tossed out, kicked out, rejected, or dropped. You have been permanently sealed as God's possession. Paul wrote:

> *"I am convinced that neither death nor life, neither angels nor demons, neither the present nor the future, nor any powers, neither height nor depth, nor anything else in all creation, will be able to separate us from the love of God that is in Christ Jesus our Lord."*
>
> — Romans 8:38-39

How blessed we are to be secure in Christ!

When you became a Christian, you became somebody. You became a new species. Your body didn't change. Your hair and eye color didn't change. You look the same and may feel the same. But you are not the same. You are a different person. Your new identity came into being at that time. You are a "new creation" (2 Corinthians 5:17). You "are God's handiwork, created in Christ Jesus" (Ephesians 2:10).

Perhaps the best way to describe your new identity is through the concept of a company.[17] Suppose there is a company that is a profit-making business; its sole purpose is to generate money for the stockholders and show a steady profit. Every employee has this goal as their purpose. Seminars are held constantly for the sales personnel, so they can increase their sales. Financial analysts work with the figures and the business plan to extract the greatest level of efficiency possible from each person and department.

One day the full ownership of the company changes hands, and it becomes a brand-new company with new leadership and a new purpose. And the new direction is to serve people rather than make money. The company's new aim is to look at the needs of the world and do something to help those who are suffering and needy. So the transition from the old way of doing business to the new way happens smoothly, right?

Wrong. All of the company's personnel, procedures, and methods of operation have been geared to the profit-making mode. Their old criteria for success is deeply ingrained, so it's time to reeducate everyone in the company. Their attitudes, beliefs, and behaviors need renovation. Even the computers need to be reprogrammed. The core of the company has changed, and this change needs to permeate every facet of the company.

The same is true of us. Before we became Christians, we lived by a deeply ingrained set of rules designed to help us get the most out of life. We were living for ourselves, not for God, and that's called sin. When we accepted Jesus Christ, we gained a totally new identity that is to be expressed in a totally new lifestyle. We are brand-new inside, but we must allow our new identity to permeate our entire being; old habits and thoughts and behaviors must change. As Romans 6:11 states: "Consider yourselves to be dead to sin, but alive to God in Christ Jesus" (NASB).

We have new directives from the new management. Romans 6:6 describes it well: "Our old self was crucified with him so that the body of sin might be done away with [rendered powerless], that we should no longer be slaves to sin."

GROWING INTO GOD'S BLESSING

Do you know what happens when you have a proper picture and understanding of God? You begin to get a proper picture and understanding of yourself. You can grow. You can be changed. You will have a solid and healthy identity.

In order to gain a clearer perception of God and how he wants to bless your life, read each statement below and then describe how you feel about it.

God is patient and available. He has chosen to spend time and attention on you (see 2 Peter 3:9).

I feel _____

_____

_____

God is kind and gracious on your behalf. He has chosen to bring help and intervention into your life (see Psalm 103:8).

I feel _____

_____

_____

God will work all things for your good. God desires
to give you his support and encouragement. You can
trust him (see Romans 8:28).

I feel _____

_____

_____

God values you as his child. He is constantly
affirming and building you up. You have value
because he created you and because you are in
Christ (see John 1:12).

I feel _____

_____

_____

God has included you in his family. You now belong to him (see Ephesians 1:4-5).

I feel _____

_____

_____

God desires intimate fellowship with you. You are valuable and priceless in his eyes (see Revelations 3:20).

I feel _____

_____

_____

God loves you just as you are. You don't have to try to earn his love (see Ephesians 2:8-9).

I feel _____

_____

_____

God accepts you regardless of your performances. He sees who you are more than what you do (see Psalm 103:8-10).

I feel _____

_____

_____

God forgives you for your sins and failures and does not hold them against you. You can be trusted to do right and to come to him when you've done wrong, knowing that he has chosen to forgive you (see 1 John 1:9).

I feel _____

_____

_____

God is just, holy, and fair. He will treat you fairly; and when he disciplines you, it will be done in love and for your own good (see Hebrews 12:5-8).

I feel _____

_____

_____

God is reliable and is with you always. He will stick
by you and support you (see Lamentations 3:22-23).

I feel _____

_____

_____

Do you struggle with feelings that you're unblessed
because of distorted images of yourself and God from
the past? Here's an exercise that will help you shed
those false perceptions and help you appreciate your
true identity and God's true nature. Write each of the
statements above, including the Scripture verses, on
a separate index card. Read this set of cards aloud to
yourself each day for two to three weeks. As you flood
your mind with God's truth, you'll be amazed at how
your perceptions of God and yourself begin to change.

FORMING AN ACCURATE VIEW
OF GOD

As already stated, an integral element in your identity is your perception of God. If your view of God is inaccurate, your view of yourself will also be inaccurate. Ideally, your overall response to God, based on a proper perception of him, will be one of trust. But many people really struggle with accepting the fact that God loves them and that he is trustworthy. Instead, they are angry at God, feeling that he failed to protect them or that he let them down. Intellectually, they may acknowledge that God is the giver of good gifts. But emotionally they perceive him as the giver of bad gifts. David Seamands describes the problem in this manner:

> When we ask individuals to trust God and to surrender to him, we are presuming they have concepts/feelings of a trustworthy God who has only their best interests at heart and in whose hands they can place their lives. But according to their deepest gut-level concept of God, they may hear us

asking them to surrender to an unpredictable and fearful ogre, an all-powerful monster whose aim is to make them miserable and take from them the freedom to enjoy life.[18]

You and I need to know the God of the Bible and use his Word as our source of information.

Transfer the basis of your identity from your other beliefs to your infallible heavenly Father. He is the one who is consistent in his love and acceptance. Note what these Scriptures say about him—and you!

> He is the loving, concerned Father who is interested in the intimate details of our lives (see Matthew 6:25-34).

> He is the Father who never gives up on us (see Luke 15:3-32).

> He is the God who sent his Son to die for us though we were undeserving (see Romans 5:8).

> He stands with us in good and bad circumstances (see Hebrews 13:5).

- He is the ever-active Creator of our universe (see Psalm 8).

- He died to heal our sickness, pain, and grief (see Isaiah 53:3-6).

- He has broken the power of death (see Luke 24:6-7).

- He gives all races and sexes equal status (see Galatians 3:28).

- He is available to us through prayer (see John 14:13-14).

- He is aware of our needs (see Isaiah 65:24).

- He created us for an eternal relationship with him (see John 3:16).

- He values us (see Luke 7:28).

- He doesn't condemn us (see Romans 8:1).

- He values and causes our growth (see 1 Corinthians 3:7).

- He comforts us (see 2 Corinthians 1:3-5).

- He strengthens us through his Spirit (see Ephesians 3:16).

- He cleanses us from sin (see Hebrews 10:17-22).

- He is for us (see Romans 8:31).

- He is always available to us (see Romans 8:38-39).

- He is a God of hope (see Romans 15:13).

- He helps us in temptation (see Hebrews 2:17-18).

- He provides a way to escape temptation (see 1 Corinthians 10:13).

- He is at work in us (see Philippians 2:13).

- He wants us to be free (see Galatians 5:1).

- He is the Lord of time and eternity (see Revelation 1:8).[19]

Read these verses aloud each day for a month. You will be amazed at how your perception of yourself will change. This really does work!

THE BASIS FOR A HEALTHY IDENTITY

Your identity is established on several foundations. First, *we all need to belong*, to know and feel that we are wanted, accepted, cared for, and enjoyed for who we are. God wants you, cares for you, accepts you, and enjoys you.

Second, *we all need to feel worthy*; we all need to be able to say with confidence, "I'm good, I'm all right, I count." We feel worthy when we do what we think we should do or when we live up to our standards. We sense worthiness in being right and doing right in our eyes and the eyes of others. God is our primary source of worthiness. We don't need to keep striving in order to feel worthy. God declares us to be all right. As professional therapist Jan Congo says, "Each of us is a divine original! We are the creative expression of a loving God!"[20]

Third, *we all need to feel competent,* knowing that we can do something and cope with life successfully. Again, God meets this need by declaring us to be competent.

Philippians 4:13 is the new measuring rod by which we are assured competence: "I can do all this through him who gives me strength."

The point here is that your identity is a gift from God. It cannot be earned through your achievements, nor is it based on what other people say about you, do to you, or fail to do to or for you.

PRACTICAL STEPS TO CHANGE

What can you do now? It is important to have the proper beliefs and a solid basis for your identity. But as you are establishing that solid foundation. It's also important to behave in a healthy new way. Here are six practical steps you can begin to take that will counter previous unhealthy ways of viewing yourself. You may want to summarize these on a sheet of paper and post it where you will read it often.

> You are still in the process of being shaped into a beautiful creation.

1. Accept the Fact That Your Are in Process

You may be dissatisfied with certain features or characteristics about your life at the present time. Realize that you are still the person God designed you to be. Yes, we have mental and physical weaknesses, we experience energy limitations, and we have needs and changing emotions. You may think you won't ever be what you want to be. But God has not completed implementing his design in you. You are still in the process of being shaped into a beautiful creation.

God knows what lies dormant within you, but he also loves you just as you are right now. He will also love you as you continue to grow and develop. Notice that I did not say he will love you more. You may think or feel that God does not love you as much today as he will when you "improve." Not true! God's love is unconditional. *He loves you!* And he wants you to cooperate with him in bringing out the best in you. He wants you to cooperate in the creative process.

Try one or both of the following activities:

ACTIVITY A

➢ On one side of a 3x5 card write the following:

"Because of Christ and his redemption, I am completely forgiven and fully pleasing to God. I am totally accepted by God."

➤ On the other side of the card, write out Romans
   5:1 and Colossians 1:21-22:

*"Therefore, since we have been justified
through faith, we have peace with God
through our Lord Jesus Christ."*

— Romans 5:1

*"Once you were alienated from God and were
enemies in your minds because of your evil
behavior. But now he has reconciled you by
Christ's physical body through death to present
you holy in his sight, without blemish and free
from accusation."*

— Colossians 1:21-22

➤ Carry this card with you for the next twenty-eight
   days. Every time you get something to drink, look
   at the card and remind yourself of what Christ has
   done for you. . . . [If you do this consistently for
   twenty-eight days, these truths will come to your
   mind for the rest of your life.] As you read and

memorize these statements and passages, think about how they apply to you. Memorization and application of these truths will have profound effects as your mind is transformed by God's Word.[21]

ACTIVITY B

➤ On one side of a 3x5 card write the word "STOP."

➤ On the other side of the card, write:

"You are worth the precious blood of Jesus."

➤ Under that sentence, write out 1 Corinthians 6:19-20; 1 Peter 1:18-19; and Revelation 5:9.

➤ Every time you find yourself thinking negatively about yourself, take the card and hold it in front of you with the word "STOP" facing you. Say the word "STOP" with emphasis and then turn the card over and read what it says. Do this as many times a day as you need to. In time these thoughts will become automatic for you.

You can hinder your growth by asking such questions as: "What will other people think?" "Will other people like me if I change?" "What if I don't please other people as much as I used to?" But you have not been called to make a good impression. Gauging your behavior by the reactions of others makes you their prisoner. It also robs you of your individuality and leads to "impression management." You end up saying what you think others want you to say, being what they want you to be, and doing what they want you to do. It is all right to be you and to develop as God wants you to develop.

2. *Affirm Yourself Instead of Tearing Yourself Down*

Jan Congo has this to say about how to avoid tearing yourself down:

> When we begin with what we have, as opposed to what we don't have, we are often surprised at how very much God has given us with which to work. Take out a pen and paper and take some time to focus on your uniqueness.

95

A. Make a list of at least 10 things you like about yourself . . . 20 things would be even better. No doubt the Lord has brought special people into your life who have helped you develop these characteristics and have affirmed your growth along the way. Put their names down beside your list.

_____

_____

_____

_____

_____

_____

_____

_____

_____

_____

_____

_____

_____

_____

_____

_____

_____

_____

_____

B. Spend time in prayer. Thank God for the 10 (or 20) things you like about yourself. Do you realize you are praising God for his creation when you do this? Then thank God for the wonderful, affirming people he has brought into your life. Finally, thank God for creating you.

C. Next, make a list of the things you honestly don't like about yourself. Go back and put a check mark beside the things you could *change* if it was important to you. . . .

_____

_____

_____

_____

_____

_____

_____

_____

_____

_____

D. The unchecked items on your list are the things about yourself that you cannot change. The time has come to thank the Lord for these and to verbalize to him your acceptance of this "thorn in your flesh." Write out an acceptance prayer to the Lord.

E. After you have written out your prayer of acceptance, covenant with the Lord not to ever again bemoan the areas you are incapable of changing.

God is limitless, but we definitely are not. By working through this exercise you choose the limitations you cannot change. You have also accepted them. This is a crucial step on your spiritual journey. Let's not waste any more time asking, "What if . . .?" If the limits on our ability can't be changed, let's accept them and accept ourselves as God does.[22]

3. *Chart the Consequences*

Keep a record of what happens when you entertain negative feelings and thoughts about yourself, and when you behave negatively. Review those consequences and ask yourself, *Is this what I really want for my life? Could I possibly believe and do the opposite of what I've written here?* Instead of dwelling on your negative thoughts, feelings, and behavior, focus on what God says about you and promises to you. For example, in Jeremiah, God says,

"Call to Me and I will answer you, and I will tell you great and mighty things, which you do not know. ... For I know the plans that I have for you, ... plans for welfare and not for calamity to give you a future and a hope."
— Jeremiah 33:3; 29:11, NASB

4. *Take New Steps*

Make a list of some special things you have always wanted to do and places you have wanted to go, activities you feel you did not deserve. Then ask someone to participate in these activities with you. Making such a request may be difficult for you at first, because it goes against your feelings about what you deserve. But do not apologize, make excuses, or give elaborate reasons. Just give it a try. After each activity, write down all your positive feelings and responses. Do not list any negative comments; only positive ones. Give yourself an opportunity to be and do something different.

5. *Saturate Yourself with the Truth of Your New Identity in Christ*

How can you grasp all the truths about who you are in Jesus Christ? How is it possible to counter the constant bombardment of your own negative messages from the past and the comments you hear in your daily life about who you are, who you should become, or what you should do? Your old, strictly human identity was molded over time in figurative concrete with a great deal of reinforcement. But alterations can occur. When you soak up the truth of who God is, what he has done for you, and who you are as a result, you will begin to be different. By saturating yourself with God's truths, you will find your new identity in Christ.

In war, saturation bombing is often used to totally obliterate enemy positions in certain areas. Planes continuously drop load after load of bombs in a back-and-forth, crisscross pattern until every inch of land has been covered. Similarly, you need to allow the Holy Spirit to saturate every inch of your heart and mind with the blessed truth of who you are and what you are becoming in Christ.

Let me tell you a story to illustrate another point about saturation. Once years ago when I was fishing in a lake, I had along with me one of my shelties. He was perched on the bow of the boat and was enjoying riding with his nose in the wind. I was headed into a cove at full speed. Then I suddenly changed my mind about fishing there, swung the boat around, and reversed direction. The sudden course change caused my dog to lose his balance, and he went flying into the lake. I don't know who was more surprised—the dog or me!

I swung the boat around and went back to where he was swimming (he wasn't too happy with me at that moment) and cut the engine. I picked him out of the water, but I didn't bring him into the boat right away, because he was totally soaked. There wasn't a dry spot of fur or skin on him. I held him away from the boat and gently squeezed his coat to eliminate most of the water.

My new dog is quite different. For one thing, he weighs three times as much as my sheltie. And since he's a golden retriever, he loves playing in the water, but he doesn't get soaked. His coat actually repels the water. When he comes out of the water, he appears wet, but the water doesn't penetrate his thick coat. After a short time, it doesn't even seem as if he even went swimming.

Some of us are thick-coated like my retriever—but in a negative way. God's truth has never thoroughly penetrated our outer layer and deeply influenced us. We haven't been fully soaked. We're not saturated with the blessing of our identity in Christ. But for growth to occur, you must saturate yourself in God's truth. How? Time and time again you will read the same instruction in this book: Take a Scripture verse or a thought that's been discussed, write it on an index card, and read it out loud to yourself morning and evening for several weeks. Spend time praying over the verse or thought, asking God to help you capture the vision of how it is to be manifested and reflected in your life. Envision yourself living out what you have read. Commit yourself by God's power to take steps to do what it says. You *will* be different.

6. *Believe What God Believes about You*

Overcoming negative feelings—whether they stem from childhood or a current situation—will take time and effort, but change *is* possible. The main step you must take in this process is to accept what your heavenly Father believes about you.

In his unique book *The Pleasures of God,* John Piper beautifully expresses how God desires to do good to all who hope in him.[23] Dr. Piper asks, "What would it be like if God sang?"

What do you hear when you imagine the voice of God singing?

I hear the booming of Niagara Falls mingled with the trickle of a mossy mountain stream. I hear the blast of Mt. Saint Helens mingled with a kitten's purr. I hear the power of an East Coast hurricane and the barely audible puff of a night snow in the woods. And I hear the unimaginable roar of the sun, 865,000 miles thick, 1,300,000 times bigger than the earth, and nothing but fire, 1,000,000 degrees centigrade on the cooler surface of the corona. But I hear this unimaginable roar mingled with the tender, warm crackling of logs in the living room on a cozy winter's night.

. . . I stand dumbfounded, staggered, speechless that he is singing over me—one who has dishonored him so many times and in so many ways. It is almost too good to be true. He is rejoicing over my good with all his heart and all his soul. He virtually breaks forth into song when he hits upon a new way to do me good.[24]

Did you catch the significance of how God feels about you and what he wants for you? Can you imagine God singing over you?

Piper compares our relationship with God to a marriage. He goes on to talk about how the honeymoon ends for all married couples. Reality sets in and the level of honeymoon intensity and affection diminishes. The two people change, and defects become more apparent. But it is different with God:

God says his joy over his people is like a bridegroom over a bride. He is talking about honeymoon intensity and honeymoon pleasures and honeymoon energy and excitement and enthusiasm and enjoyment. He is trying to get into our hearts what he means when he says he rejoices over us *with all his heart.*

And to add to this, that with God the honeymoon never ends. He is infinite in power and wisdom and creativity and love. And so he has no trouble sustaining a honeymoon level of intensity, he can foresee all the future quirks of our personality and has decided he will keep what's good for us and change what isn't. [25]

Does that say something to you about your value and worth? Does that fling open the doors of possibility for you? It can!

You have the rest of your life ahead of you. Experience it with your new identity.

Enjoy it, for it's God's gift to you!

Notes

1 *No One*, 1970, by Linda Rich. Used by permission (Intervarsity Christian Fellowship of the USA).

2 Judith Viorst, *Necessary Losses: The Loves, Illusions, Dependencies, and Impossible Expectations That All of Us Have to Give Up in Order to Grow* (New York: Simon and Schuster, 1986).

3 For more information about dreams and identity, see R. Scott Sullender, *Losses in Later Life: A New Way of Walking with God* (New York: Paulist Press, 1989).

4 Jan Congo, *Free to Be God's Woman: Building a Solid Foundation for a Healthy Self-Image* (Ventura, CA: Regal Books, 1988), p. 27.

5 Jordan and Margaret Paul, *If You Really Loved Me* (Minneapolis, MN: CompCare Publications, 1987), pp. 127-28.

6 Original source unknown.

7 Lloyd John Ogilvie, *Lord of the Impossible* (Nashville, TN: Abingdon Press, 1984), pp. 129-30.

8 Robert S. McGee, *The Search for Significance*, rev. ed. (Nashville, TN: W Publishing Group, 1998, 2003), pp. 84-85.

9 *Healing Grace for Hurting People* (Ventura, CA: Regal Books, 2007, pp. 34-46, adapted.

10 Phillip Yancey, *What's So Amazing about Grace?* (Grand Rapids, MI: Zondervan, 1997), p. 70.

11 John Ortberg, *Love Beyond Reason: Moving God from Your Head to Your Heart* (Grand Rapids, MI: Zondervan, 1998), p. 139.

12 David Seamands, *Healing Grace* (Colorado Springs, CO: Victor Books, 1988), p. 115.

13 McGee, *Search for Significance*, p. 266.

14 Don Colbert, *Deadly Emotions: Understand the Mind-Body-Spirit Connection That Can Heal or Destroy You* (Nashville, TN: Thomas Nelson, 2003), pp. 147-48, quoted in H. Norman Wright and Larry Renetzky, *Healing Grace for Hurting People* (Ventura, CA: Regal Books, 2007), p. 46.

15 Ibid.

16 Much of what follows in this section originally appeared in H. Norman Wright, *Chosen for Blessing: Discover Your Unsearchable Riches in Christ* (Eugene, OR: Harvest House Publishers, 1992), pp. 36-38.

17 The idea of comparing an individual to a company originated in David C. Needham, *Birthright* (Portland, OR: Multnomah Press, 1979), pp. 127–29.

18 David Seamands, *Healing of Memories* (Wheaton, IL: Victor Books, 1985). p. 11.

19 H. Norman Wright, *Always Daddy's Girl: Understanding Your Father's Impact on Who You Are* (Ventura, CA: Regal Books, 1989), pp. 196-97

20 Congo, *Free to Be God's Woman*, p. 95.

21 McGee, *The Search for Significance*, p. 94.

22 Congo, *Free to Be God's Woman*, pp. 96-98.

23 Much of what follows in this section originally appeared in H. Norman Wright, *Chosen for Blessing: Discover Your Unsearchable Riches in Christ* (Eugene, OR: Harvest House, 1992), pp. 14-15.

24 John Piper, *The Pleasures of God: Meditations on God's Delight in Being God* (Portland, OR: Multnomah, 1991), p. 87.

25 Ibid., p. 95.

Other titles by Dr. Norm Wright

Helping Your Hurting Teen

Is your teen withdrawing, acting unusual, sullen or distracted? Do you feel like you just don't know your child anymore? Are you afraid it's more than just a stage? Learn which responses are "normal" adolescent behaviors, and which ones indicate deeper issues related to loss or trauma. Expert Dr. Norm Wright gives insight on how to reconnect with your child, understand their struggle, and never lose hope. **ISBN 9781628620542**

Recovering from the Loss of a Love

How do you cope when someone you love walks away from you? Whether it is the agony of unrequited love or the loss of a breakup, this book helps you move through the stages of grief and loss, and guides you toward wholeness and hope. Author Dr. Norm Wright compassionately and practically helps you work through the feeling of loss, grief, and rejection.
ISBN 9781628620580

Overcoming Fear and Worry

When anxiety robs your sleep, when worry saps your energy, and when fear captivates your thoughts, it is easy to feel helpless. But you do not have to remain a prisoner of fear, anxiety, or stress any longer. Dr. Norm Wright helps you combat negative thought patterns with the Word of God and gives you practical ways to develop resilience in the face of trials through positive self-talk.
ISBN 9781628620627

HOPE FOR THE HEART
Biblical Counseling Library

Anger	Forgiveness	Verbal & Emotional Abuse	Depression
ISBN 9781596366411	ISBN 9781596366435	ISBN 9781596366459	ISBN 9781596366497

The Bible is full of good advice, but often we don't remember what passages are the best or what Christian counselors recommend. These minibooks by 20-year veteran radio host June Hunt are packed with biblical wisdom, practical advice, and real solutions for the problems Christians face every day. They offer hope—and are affordable enough to give away to those in crisis. There are 48 titles available.

Who can use these:
- People who want to help a hurting friend
- Pastoral counselors and church leaders
- Small group Bible study and care group leaders
- Mentors and life coaches

How to use:
- Personal use or giving to a friend in need
- Small groups and Sunday school classes
- Grief and bereavement, and recovery groups
- Visitation – There's a title for nearly every problem

"After decades of counseling men and women from all walks of life, June knows how to lead readers to truth – truth that liberates because it is truth from God."

Kay Arthur, Co-founder of Precept Ministries International and author of *When the Hurt Runs Deep*